Christmas Programs

FOR THE

Church

compiled by

Pat Fittro

Standard
PUBLISHING
CINCINNATI, OHIO

Permission is granted to reproduce these programs
for ministry purposes only—not for resale.

Standard Publishing, Cincinnati, Ohio
A division of Standex International Corporation
© 2003 by Standard Publishing

ISBN 0-7847-1310-3

Contents

No Room

Judith A. Hupp and Brenda J. Hupp

Summary and staging information

Scene 1: The Tyler children are gathered in the kitchen. Sissy, the eldest, is making a sandwich for her supper. Butch and Bonnie, the younger siblings, are bickering. Widowed father, Marcus is at his desk in his study, studiously ignoring the family rabble while he pays the bills. Grandmother, Catherine, wades into the typical confusion filleting it with her shrill criticism. Her expertly aimed prods draw a reluctant Marcus into the fray, creating a depressingly habitual war-zone family evening. Catherine's matriarchal scepter has fallen on a noncompliant Marcus, so she clings to the lingering shreds of figurehead authority as she leaves the family battleground for the grocery store.

Scene 2: Young widow, Jane Tyler, and her daughter, Mary, are wandering the snowy street of an unfamiliar city, searching for the home of Marcus Tyler. With the cold and darkness pressing in on them, Jane desperately accosts Catherine as she exits the grocery store. Suspicious and cynical, Catherine is sure Jane is after her money, but her icy heart is touched by a haunting familiarity at the sight of little Mary's face. A hostile Catherine points the way to the Tyler house without revealing her identity.

Scene 3: Catherine arrives home just moments before Jane and Mary knock on the door. When Marcus is summoned to greet the new arrivals, his jaded attitude and rancorous questioning immediately put an already nervous Jane on edge. Her efforts to speak to Marcus privately stir up his anger. The Tyler children join in the verbal barrage, further inciting their father's wrath, which he takes out on Jane and Mary, ordering them out of the house. Catherine intervenes, using the stormy night as a valid excuse for allowing Jane and Mary to stay.

Marcus retreats into his fortress of solitude study while the excited Tyler siblings pump Jane and Mary for any tidbit of Christmas cheer. Their drab non-celebration of the holiday takes on a rare festive air when Jane shares the true meaning of Christmas and teaches them a carol to sing.

After the children go to bed, Catherine interrogates Jane to discover what she already suspects, that Jane is the widowed wife of her recently deceased eldest grandson, Matthew Tyler. Marcus, eavesdropping on their conversation, is angry and upset by Jane's revelation, and lashes out at his newly found daughter-in-law. Unleashing his own frustrations and guilt about his long-ago argument and falling out with his eldest son, Matthew, Marcus loses all perspective of time and human relationships. As he did with Matthew six years prior, he orders Jane and Mary to leave his house and never return. Catherine offers Jane her support and prays for a way to reach an embittered Marcus.

Scene 4: The Tyler children are getting ready for bed. Sissy frantically searches through her closet until she finds her grandmother's old Bible. The children read the Christmas story from Luke 2 and talk about this unfamiliar message from the first Christmas.

Scene 5: Jane enters the Tyler girls' bedroom to tuck in Mary. She finds Sissy still awake, poring over the Bible, searching for answers. Sissy assaults Jane with questions, becoming angry when she asks Jane why God allowed Matthew to be killed in an accident. Jane offers no pat answer, which frustrates Sissy all the more. Jane points Sissy to the ultimate answer to all life's questions: personal faith in Christ.

Scene 6: The following morning, Jane and Mary prepare to leave, despite the protests of the Tyler siblings and Catherine. Before she goes, Jane places a wrapped present for Marcus under the cardboard Christmas tree. The Tyler children try to convince Marcus to let Jane and Mary stay. When he won't relent on his ultimatum, his own family turns against him and the children chase after Jane and Mary out into the street.

Catherine cuts Marcus to the quick, criticizing his parenting skills, and warning him about the very real possibility of losing his children one by one, just as he destroyed his relationship with Matthew. Marcus deflects the criticism and advice by throwing it back in his mother's face. Catherine urges him to let the past go and seek God's help.

Jane, Mary, and the Tyler children return. Jane stands up to Marcus and reveals her true reason for coming to the house. She gives Marcus the gift of a Bible, selected by Matthew before he died. Marcus refuses to accept the gift, but wearily gives in to his children's arguments and agrees to let Jane and Mary stay for Christmas.

Scene 7: Still operating on her burst of courage, Jane follows Marcus, breaching the lonely security of his study. She wants to force him to accept Matthew's gift, but Marcus is adamant in his refusal. Angrily, he spits out all his pent-up rage at losing his eldest son. When Jane attempts to offer comfort and share her faith, Marcus verbally attacks her beliefs. Raw with grief and frustration, Jane gives vent to the harsh truth, telling Marcus he got what he deserved. By cutting off his son while he was still alive, and refusing to allow Matthew to heal the breach with his family, Marcus had acted as if his son were already dead. During Jane's tirade, she tells Marcus maybe he got what he wanted. Now Matthew really is dead and that is God's wake-up call. Appalled at what she has said, Jane apologizes, but Marcus freezes her out.

Scene 8: On Christmas morning, the children are excited, but Jane is sickened by her argument with Marcus. Marcus distributes Christmas presents, as though nothing unusual has occurred. When Catherine sees selfish Butch giving his unopened gifts to Jane and Mary, she points out a marked similarity to Matthew. Marcus is just about to return Matthew's Bible once more to Jane when the reality of hope and the possibility of change become real to his heart. He vows to keep the Bible and then invites Jane and Mary to stay and become part of his family. Marcus accepts his role as son, parent, and grandparent, and asks Jane to help him understand Matthew's life and his faith.

Characters:

JANE TYLER—A young Christian woman with a good heart and good intentions, she must find the courage and faith to carry out her promise to her dead husband, Matthew, and reveal the secret she carries with her.

MARY TYLER—Four-year-old daughter of Jane and Matthew Tyler; although she is shy, she knows the joy and the true meaning of Christmas.

MARCUS TYLER—A crusty widower, who argued with his oldest son, Matthew, several years ago, Matthew left and they never spoke again. Now Matthew is dead, killed in an Army training accident. Marcus' guilt has caused him to be angry with God. He has no patience and no hope for the future.

CATHERINE TYLER—Mother of Marcus, she is old and tired, believing she no longer has a place in the life of her family; she is bitter and ready to go into a nursing home and die.

SISSY TYLER—Seventeen-year-old daughter of Marcus, she pretends to be happy all the time. She is always busy and, like the cheerleader she is, tries to enforce artificial joy on the rest of the family members.

BONNIE TYLER—Thirteen-year-old daughter of Marcus; a brainy student, she shuts herself away from the rest of the family, spending most of her time with her nose stuck in a book, except when she bickers with her brother, Butch.

BUTCH TYLER—Ten-year-old and youngest of the Tyler children, he picks arguments with everyone, trying to force the other family members to pay attention to him. When they ignore him, he gets his revenge in acts of jealousy, selfishness, and greed.

OTHER SHOPPERS

Scripture are from the *Holy Bible, New International Version.*

Scene 1

It is early evening at the Tyler home two days before Christmas. Marcus is sitting at his desk paying bills. Sissy is making a sandwich. Bonnie is reading. Butch enters and purposely beans his sister Bonnie with the sponge ball he is tossing.

BONNIE: Butch, quit it!
BUTCH: It was an accident. Don't be such a crybaby.
BONNIE: You did it on purpose

BUTCH: Did not.

BONNIE: Did too.

BUTCH: Did not. Did not. Did not.

BONNIE: Did too. Did too. Did too.

SISSY: Stop it you two.

BUTCH: Did not. *(Picks up and throws ball at Bonnie. She gets up and chases him around the table.)*

BONNIE: Did too, to infinity.

SISSY: I said stop it. It's almost Christmas; can't you stop bickering for just one day, for crying out loud?

BUTCH: You're not the boss of me, Sissy.

(Catherine Tyler enters the room.)

CATHERINE: What's going on here?

SISSY: I was making supper for myself. Would you like something, Gram?

(Catherine looks at the peanut butter and jelly and frowns. Butch and Bonnie each grab the ball and are fighting and arguing in the background.)

CATHERINE: We ought to have a regular sit-down supper at night like normal people. *(Raises her voice to shrill.)* Are you listening, Marcus?

MARCUS: Ma, how could I not hear what you are saying? Please don't start up with me again. You know my work schedule doesn't allow me to have set hours.

CATHERINE: You're here right now, aren't you? What's the matter with eating together tonight?

(Marcus reluctantly leaves his desk and leans in from the adjoining room. Butch and Bonnie get louder with their exchange of "It's mine, give it to me!" until that is all you can hear.)

MARCUS *(raising his voice over the children):* I can't, OK? I'm trying to pay these bills. You all think I'm made of money.

CATHERINE: But look at our family. We're falling apart.

MARCUS (*strides over and grabs the ball out of Butch and Bonnie's hands and growls*): Go find something quiet to do. Right now!

(*Bonnie goes back to reading. Butch snatches the ball out of his father's hand and starts tossing it and catching it over Bonnie's head again.*)

CATHERINE: Marcus.

MARCUS: Ma, I said stay out of it. This is my family. I take care of them and you. Don't tell me how to do my job.

CATHERINE: Is that all we are to you is a job? I guess I'm just an old woman. I don't want to be a burden.

MARCUS: Ma, don't get into your "just put me in a home" speech again. I'm not in the mood for your martyrdom. I don't have time.

(*Catherine turns around in a huff and puts on her coat.*)

CATHERINE: I am going into a home, Marcus, and you can't stop me. I'm no good to anyone here. I'm useless. I might as well go into a nursing home and wait to die. (*She turns away from Marcus and puts on her overcoat and grabs her cane. Sissy chases after her and grabs her arm.*)

MARCUS: Ma, please don't pull this garbage on me tonight.

(*He shakes his head, runs an agitated hand through his hair and trudges back to his desk. Bonnie and Butch start to fight again.*)

SISSY: Gram, you aren't really going to leave us, are you?

CATHERINE: Not tonight, Sissy. Right now I'm going to the grocery store.

MARCUS (*raising his voice*): You don't need to go to the store, Ma. I'll get groceries tomorrow.

CATHERINE (*leaving*): We need them now!

Scene 2

Outside a grocery store in town, Jane Tyler walks down the street holding Mary's hand. Both have on coats and backpacks and they shiver in the cold while Jane searches for an address.

JANE: We'll find it soon, Mary. Are you warm enough? *(Mary shakes her head no. Catherine comes up the street with a grocery bag.)* Excuse me.

(Catherine stops and fixes a suspicious eye on Jane and Mary. Other shoppers rush by and jostle Catherine. Jane reaches out to steady her, but Catherine jerks away from her touch.)

CATHERINE: You'll keep your hands off me if you know what's good for you. If you think I'm an easy target because I'm old, you're wrong! I have a cane and I know how to use it. *(Lifts her cane menacingly.)*

JANE: No, please; you misunderstood. I'm not here to steal from you.

CATHERINE: If you think I'm going to give you a handout, you're mistaken. I have barely enough money for myself. You're young and strong. What's the matter with you? You ought to be out working instead of trying to bum money from old people.

JANE: I don't want your money. I simply wanted to ask you for directions. Do you know where Marcus Tyler lives?

CATHERINE: Why do you want to know?

JANE: Uh, I . . . I need to see him.

CATHERINE: And who are you?

JANE: My name is Jane and this is Mary.

CATHERINE *(squints down at Mary):* The little girl looks familiar. Do I know you?

JANE: I don't think so, but you haven't told me your name.

CATHERINE: That's because it's none of your business. *(Starts to leave.)*

JANE *(calling after her):* Please! Do you know where Marcus Tyler lives? My daughter is very cold and tired. I need your help.

(Catherine turns and looks her up and down for a moment.)

No Room

CATHERINE: I don't know if I should help you or not.

JANE: Please, if you can't help me, or won't, couldn't you at least tell me where I might find a room nearby for the night? I just found out the buses are no longer running tonight because of the storm.

CATHERINE *(snappish and hurried as if she is angry with herself for giving in to Jane's pleading):* Marcus Tyler lives at 85 Greenwood Street. Take your next right, go two blocks and turn left. It's the white house on the hill.

JANE: Thank you.

CATHERINE: Don't thank me. I don't trust you. You remember that.

(Catherine exits. Jane adjusts Mary's hat and mittens.)

JANE: What an odd woman! Still, she was an answer to our prayers, wasn't she? *(Mary shakes her head yes.)* We'll be warm soon and we'll have Christmas with our new family, you'll see. God is looking out for us. *(They leave.)*

Scene 3

The Tyler home on the same evening, Marcus is still at his desk. Bonnie is reading at the table with her hands over her ears. Butch has stolen Sissy's sandwich and is eating it while still managing to irritate both his sisters. Sissy hears an insistent cane banging on the outside door, crosses to the portal and opens it. Catherine enters. Sissy takes the grocery bag and helps her grandmother inside.

SISSY: Gram, are you all right? You were gone a long time. I was worried when I noticed it had started snowing again.

CATHERINE: It's very cold out there, not a fit night to be out. Turn on the teakettle and put on some soup.

SISSY: You hate soup.

CATHERINE: Don't give me any back talk. Just do as I say.

(Sissy hurries to obey her grandmother. A knock sounds at the door. Bonnie answers the door but her grandmother is right behind her. Jane and Mary are outside.)

JANE: Hello, is this Marcus Tyler's home?
BONNIE: Yes, it is.
JANE: May we come in please?
BONNIE: I guess so. *(Yells.)* Dad there's someone here to see you.

(Jane and Mary enter and suddenly Jane notices Catherine standing nearby.)

JANE: It's you! Who are you?
CATHERINE: I still don't see that it's any of your business.

(Marcus enters.)

MARCUS *(speaking to Jane):* What do you want?

(The family gathers around and stares at Jane and Mary.)

JANE: Mr. Tyler, is there somewhere we could talk privately?
MARCUS: Why? Who are you?
JANE: I'm Jane and this is Mary. It's important I speak with you in private.
MARCUS: Oh no you don't! I've heard all about your kind on the news. This is some kind of Christmas shakedown, isn't it? You come into my home looking cold and hungry and you con me into giving you money. You tell me the kid won't have any presents and you expect me to feel all guilty and sympathetic because I have money and you don't.
JANE: No, no you've got it all wrong! I'm here to give you something.
MARCUS: Yeah, right! You expect me to believe that line? We're strangers. I don't know you. You force yourself into my home on a dark, snowy night and you expect me to believe you don't want anything from me?
JANE: Well, I was hoping we could stay, just until my daughter gets warm.

MARCUS: That's what I thought! The kid's a nice touch, but it won't work! Get out of my house.

SISSY: But Dad, it's Christmas. *(Sissy kneels down and takes off Mary's mittens and starts to warm the little girl's hands.)*

MARCUS: Christmas, Smasmas, who cares? I have enough to do supporting my own family. She's not my responsibility. *(Pointing to Jane.)* Look, whoever you are, there's a homeless shelter across town. If you really need a place to stay for the night, which I seriously doubt, you can go there.

(Marcus walks across to the door ushering Jane and Mary in front of him.)

CATHERINE: It's too stormy for her to walk all the way across town tonight. She'll have to stay here.

MARCUS: There are buses or taxis. She can hitchhike for all I care. It's not my problem.

JANE: Please, if you would just give me a chance to explain.

CATHERINE *(walks over and stands between Jane and the door and faces Marcus):* She must stay here for tonight. It's stormy and the buses have stopped running.

MARCUS: Ma, have you lost your mind? Maybe it is time for you to move into that nursing home you're always talking about. You have no right to interfere with my decisions. This is my house in case you have forgotten. *(Marcus storms out past Catherine and Jane.)*

JANE: I'm so sorry. I didn't mean to cause an argument.

SISSY: It's okay. It happens all the time. Dad will get over it someday. Come in and have something to eat.

(Sissy takes their coats and leads them into the kitchen. Mary pulls on Jane's arm and whispers something in her ear.)

CATHERINE: Mary doesn't say much, does she?

JANE: She will once she gets to know you.

BUTCH: She won't get the chance. Is everyone here deaf? In case you didn't hear, Dad just kicked you out.

SISSY: Be quiet, Butch.

BUTCH: I'd like to see you make me.

CATHERINE: Butch, you're a tattletale and a troublemaker. I have no use for either tonight. You can stay here and be still or go to your room.

BUTCH: But, Gram . . .

CATHERINE *(giving Butch a quelling look):* I said be still!

JANE: He's right.

(Butch gets a smug look on his face but instantly wipes it off when he catches his grandmother's thundercloud expression.)

CATHERINE: Pay no attention to my grandson or my son. Both have taken leave of their senses, momentarily.

(Mary whispers in Jane's ear.)

BONNIE: What did she say?

JANE: She wants to know why you don't have any Christmas decorations.

SISSY: We never have a tree. Gram says it is too much bother and it makes the house too messy.

BUTCH: We don't wrap presents either.

BONNIE: Dad says it's a waste of time and money.

SISSY: We used to do all that stuff, but when Mom died and our brother Matthew left, Dad didn't want to celebrate anything anymore.

BONNIE: Yeah, before Matthew left, he and Dad had a huge fight.

BUTCH: Matthew's never coming back.

CATHERINE: He's dead; killed in a training accident in the Army. God has been cruel to this family. We have nothing to celebrate, least of all Christmas.

SISSY: We do have something to celebrate this year. Jane and Mary are here and I'm glad they came.

JANE: Thank you.

SISSY: I'm going to put up some decorations Bonnie and I made last year.

(Sissy and Bonnie exit and return with a cardboard Christmas tree and some paper snowflakes.)

BUTCH: That's ugly.

BONNIE: It is not!

BUTCH: Is too!

JANE: It's nice, but Christmas is more than decorations.

BUTCH: It's all about presents!

JANE: Do you know who gave the first Christmas present?

BUTCH: No, but I'm sure it wasn't my dad.

JANE: It happened way before your dad was born. God gave us the very first Christmas present. God sent His only Son, Christ, to earth. On Christmas we celebrate Christ's birthday.

SISSY: Gram used to read us the story of baby Jesus in a manger, do you remember?

BONNIE: I do.

BUTCH: I don't! Is it important?

JANE: It's the most important thing on earth. Without Jesus there would be no Christmas.

BUTCH AND BONNIE: Why?

JANE: Because Jesus is God's gift to each one of us. Jesus came to show us our lives have meaning here, and that life doesn't end when we die.

CATHERINE: I used to believe that.

SISSY: You did?

CATHERINE: Yes, I still believe your grandfather is in Heaven waiting for me.

JANE: Jesus came to earth to show each of you how much God loves you.

SISSY: God loves me?

JANE: Yes, God loves every one of us.

BUTCH: Even Dad?

JANE: Yes, even your dad. I know a song about Christmas. We used to sing it together every Christmas. I wasn't sure I'd be able to sing it this year, but I think I'd like to try. Mary, will you help me?

(Jane is nearly in tears. Mary nods and takes her mother's hand. Everyone gathers around the cardboard Christmas tree. Jane and Mary sing the old classic "C-H-R-I-S-T-M-A-S" by Jenny Lou Carson.)

SISSY: I like that.

BONNIE: Me, too. Can we sing it with you?

BUTCH: I think singing is stupid.

BONNIE: You would! You hate everything because you're hateful.

(Catherine gives the bickering children a scowl and opens her mouth to scold.)

JANE *(hurriedly intervening):* Let's sing it again. Together this time.

(The others join in the song and even Butch begins to mouth the words.)

CATHERINE: Time for everyone to go to bed.

SISSY: But we want to stay up and talk to Jane.

CATHERINE: You can talk with her tomorrow. Everyone to bed now.

SISSY, BONNIE, AND BUTCH: Good night, Jane.

JANE: Good night. *(Jane gives Mary a hug.)* Sweet dreams. I'll be in to tuck you in and hear your prayers in a minute.

SISSY: Good night, Gram. Come on, Mary. I'll help you get ready for bed.

(Sissy takes Mary's hand and Butch and Bonnie follow as they exit to the bedrooms.)

JANE: I ought to see to Mary myself.

(Jane starts to rise but Catherine puts a detaining hand on the younger woman's arm.)

CATHERINE: Not so fast! Sissy is a good girl. She can take care of Mary for a little while. You have some explaining to do first. Who are you?

JANE: I think I should wait and talk to Mr. Tyler.

CATHERINE: Your little girl looks awfully familiar. *(Catherine picks up a photo from the table.)* In fact, she's the spitting image of my grandson, Matthew, when he was small.

(Marcus comes in quietly and stands by the door, eavesdropping on the conversation.)

JANE *(studies the picture with her head bent, as if praying for strength, then looks straight at Catherine):* Mary does favor her father.

CATHERINE: I thought so! You are Matthew's wife.

JANE: Yes. We'd planned to come here together. Even though Matthew died, I know he wanted me to keep our promise to come here for Christmas.

CATHERINE: Why didn't you tell Marcus right away?

JANE: I tried, but the words wouldn't come. I wanted to tell him, but I was afraid. After his accusations and eviction, he didn't give me a chance. I didn't understand why Matthew couldn't heal the breach with his father. I thought he should talk to his father, say he was sorry. The solution seemed so easy.

CATHERINE: Things are never easy with this family.

JANE: Matthew told me his father was a proud and stubborn man. I didn't know it would be so hard to tell Mr. Tyler the truth.

(Marcus strides in and confronts them.)

MARCUS: Do you want to know the truth? Here's the truth! My son Matthew is dead! I'll never see him again. I'll never talk to him again.

JANE: That's not true, Mr. Tyler. Matthew believed in Jesus as his personal Savior. When he died, he went to Heaven.

MARCUS: I don't believe it.

JANE: But you can! Just like Matthew, you can believe Jesus died on the cross for your sins.

MARCUS: Quiet! I don't need you to tell me about my sins, and I don't want you and your little daughter around to constantly remind me of them!

JANE: I came here to give you something. Matthew wanted you to have it.

MARCUS: No. I don't want anything from Matthew or from you. Matthew told you I was proud and stubborn, did he? Well, he was right. I threw him out of this house six years ago. Why would you think I would welcome you into my home now?

JANE: Mary has a right to know her family. She just lost her father. She needs her grandfather and great-grandmother.

MARCUS: My son is dead. I have no son. I have no daughter-in-law or granddaughter. I want you out of here by morning. If you don't go willingly, I'll call the cops.

CATHERINE: Marcus! *(Marcus stomps out of the room. Catherine puts her arm around Jane.)* He didn't mean it.

JANE: Yes, he did.

CATHERINE: Go to bed now and rest. Things will be better in the morning.

(Jane nods, then retrieves a Christmas gift—a Bible wrapped in holiday paper—out of her backpack and places it under the tree. She kneels and prays. Catherine watches her and then bows her head in prayer too.)

Scene 4

The scene opens the same evening in Bonnie and Sissy's bedroom. The room is messy, toys, books, and clothes are scattered everywhere. Bonnie is on her bed reading. Sissy is rooting around in her closet with Mary hunkered down beside her, watching every move she makes. Butch enters. All are dressed in nightwear and/or bathrobes.

BUTCH: What are you doing, Sissy?

BONNIE *(lowers her book and scowls):* You're not supposed to be in here, Butch. Get back to bed.

BUTCH *(comes over and flops down on the foot of Bonnie's bed and continues to jar and bounce the bed to aggravate his sister):* You can't make me.

BONNIE *(grabs her pillow and takes a swing at Butch):* Get off my bed!

(Butch laughs and grabs the pillow. Mary sits on the floor and covers her ears.)

Sissy: Stop it, Butch! You're scaring Mary.

Butch: It's not my fault. Bonnie started it!

Bonnie: Did not!

Sissy: I said quit it! Do you want Dad to come in here? He's in a more rotten mood than usual and I don't think he's gotten any presents for you yet, if you know what I mean.

Butch *(immediately drops the pillow and sits down carefully on the foot of the bed, cross-legged with his elbows on his knees, chin resting in his hands):* A Christmas with no presents, what a bummer!

Bonnie: Dad will get you something anyway, even if you haven't been good. He always does, and you're never good.

Butch: Yeah, you're right. *(Mary gets up and comes over and sits beside him on the bed.)* But what about Mary? *(He lowers his voice to a loud stage whisper.)* She might not get anything for Christmas.

Bonnie: Butch! Don't you think she heard that?

Butch: Sorry, Mary. I didn't mean it. I'll see you get a present, even if I have to give you one of mine.

Bonnie: Butch! You're only making things worse. Be quiet!

Sissy *(backing out of the closet in triumph with a Bible in her hand):* I found it!

(The other children look at her.)

Butch: What is it?

Sissy: Christmas. It's what Jane was talking about. Forget about presents for a minute. They're not important. I just hope I can remember . . . *(Sissy thoughtfully searches through the pages in the Bible until she locates Luke chapter two. She looks at the others and smiles.)* I have it! This is the Christmas story that Gram used to read to Matthew and me.

Bonnie: Let me read it! *(Reaches out to grab the Bible from her sister, then stops.)* Please, Sissy? I could read it aloud for all of us.

(Sissy hands Bonnie the Bible and they all gather on the bed around Bonnie.)

BONNIE: "In those days Caesar Augustus issued a decree that a census should be taken of the entire Roman world. (This was the first census that took place while Quirinius was governor of Syria.) And everyone went to his own town to register. So Joseph also went up from the town of Nazareth in Galilee to Judea, to Bethlehem the town of David, because he belonged to the house and line of David. He went there to register with Mary, who was pledged to be married to him and was expecting a child. While they were there, the time came for the baby to be born, and she gave birth to her first-born, a son. She wrapped him in cloths and placed him in a manger, because there was no room for them in the inn. And there were shepherds living out in the fields nearby, keeping watch over their flocks at night. An angel of the Lord appeared to them, and the glory of the Lord shone around them, and they were terrified. But the angel said to them, 'Do not be afraid. I bring you good news of great joy that will be for all people. Today in the town of David a Savior has been born to you; he is Christ the Lord. This will be a sign to you: You will find a baby wrapped in cloths and lying in a manger.' Suddenly a great company of the heavenly host appeared with the angel, praising God and saying, 'Glory to God in the highest, and on earth peace to men on whom his favor rests.' When the angels had left them and gone into heaven, the shepherds said to one another. 'Let's go to Bethlehem and see this thing that has happened, which the Lord has told us about.' So they hurried off and found Mary and Joseph, and the baby, who was lying in the manger. When they had seen him, they spread the word concerning what had been told them about this child, and all who heard it were amazed at what the shepherds said to them. But Mary treasured up all these things and pondered them in her heart. The shepherds returned, glorifying and praising God for all the things they had heard and seen, which were just as they had been told" (Luke 2:1-20).

(Stage goes dark.)

Scene 5

Bonnie and Sissy's bedroom, same evening. When the lights come up Bonnie is asleep in her bed. Mary is asleep next to Sissy who is reading the Bible. Jane enters, crosses to the bed, and kisses Mary lightly on the forehead.

JANE: I thought you'd be asleep.

SISSY: I just got the little kids to sleep a few minutes ago. We read the story of Jesus' birth from Gram's old Bible. Butch and Bonnie had a lot of questions. I did my best to answer them, but I didn't have all the answers.

JANE: No one does.

SISSY: Oh. *(Looking dejected.)* You know about Jesus, so I thought you knew the answers. I was hoping you could help me.

JANE *(sits on the bed beside Sissy):* I can try. What do you want to know?

SISSY: Was Matthew happy, truly happy inside?

JANE: Yes, he was, but I know he missed you.

SISSY: I miss him too.

JANE: I miss him so much too; so much sometimes it hurts. *(Jane puts a comforting hand on Sissy's shoulder.)* I wish he was still alive, but God had a plan for Matthew's life here and hereafter, and He has a plan for our lives too.

SISSY: You really believe that, don't you? *(Jane nods, takes Sissy's hand in hers and squeezes it.)* Why would God let Matthew be born just to have him die so young? Why did God allow Jesus to be born in a stable just to grow up to die on a cross? *(Sissy closes the Bible and hangs her head.)* I don't understand.

JANE: It's all about love. God loves you and He wants to have a personal relationship with you.

SISSY: But I don't know how!

JANE: That's why God sent His Son to earth. Jesus is "God with us." He is both God and man, the Unique Person of the universe. Jesus shows us the way to connect with God.

SISSY: By dying?

JANE: By living. Jesus died on the cross as our substitute, but He didn't die a meaningless death. He died to save us from sin, and He rose from the dead to give us eternal life with Him. If you trust in Jesus as your Savior, you can know what it means to be free from sin and death.

SISSY: And Matthew believed this?

JANE: Yes.

SISSY: But he died.

JANE: Yes. *(Jane bows her head for a moment, then raises it and looks intently at Sissy.)* I wish Matthew was here with us right now, but he's not. He's in Heaven.

SISSY: You're sure?

JANE: I'm positive. You know, even though it was only for a short while, I wouldn't change my time with Matthew for anything. Our love was a gift from God. Without Matthew, I wouldn't have Mary, and I might never have met all of you.

SISSY *(frustrated):* But why couldn't Matthew have been here too? *(At her angry tone, Mary tosses in her sleep. Jane reaches over and runs a soothing hand over her daughter's hair. Sissy lowers her voice to a hiss.)* Why did he have to die?

JANE: I can't give you the answer you want to hear. I'd like to be able to say something that would take away all the hurt, but the only way I know how to do that is to tell you God loves Matthew. God has a reason I don't fully understand for taking Matthew from us. Some day I'll understand; in the meantime, I know God is going to work out this sorrow for our good, Mary's and mine.

SISSY: What about me? Don't I count? I read over and over what the angel said. Jesus birth was "good news of great joy" for all people. I'm a person, too! Why don't I have a great joy? Why doesn't our family have any joy at all? Are we that bad?

JANE *(giving Sissy a hug):* No. God knows you by name, Sissy. He's loved you forever. He wants to give you His love and joy, but it's like a gift under the Christmas tree. It's there for you; all you need to do is accept it and open it for yourself. No one can do it for you. Jesus isn't in the manger or on the cross anymore. He's waiting for you to ask Him into your heart. That's where the joy and love start.

Scene 6

The Tyler home the next morning. Butch and Bonnie are looking at the wrapped present Jane placed under the cardboard tree last night. Mary and Jane enter with their coats and backpacks on, followed by Sissy and Catherine.

SISSY: Please, Jane, don't go. I'll talk to Dad and make him understand.

JANE *(puts her arm around Sissy):* It'll be all right, Sissy. Mary and I can't stay if it upsets your father. Perhaps things will be better after Christmas and we'll come back.

BONNIE *(comes over to stand in front of Jane, Butch is close behind):* No, Jane, you and Mary can't leave, not now.

BUTCH: We made a Christmas present for you.

(Bonnie and Butch hand Jane a drawing of the manger scene.)

BONNIE: I read the true story of Christmas last night.

BUTCH: And we drew a picture of the first real Christmas when Jesus was born.

JANE: It's beautiful. Mary and I will think of you every time we look at it. Thank you.

(Marcus enters and frowns.)

BONNIE *(races over, picks up the present under the tree and reads the tag aloud):* "To Dad. Merry Christmas. Love, Matthew, Jane, and Mary." Jane brought you a real Christmas present, Dad.

MARCUS: What do you mean a real Christmas present? I buy you real Christmas presents every year.

BUTCH: No you don't! You only buy us stuff so we won't bug you.

SISSY: You don't really care about us.

MARCUS *(pointing an accusing finger at Jane):* See what you started? This is all your fault. I want you out of my home and away from my family, now!

SISSY: Gram! Do something, please!

CATHERINE: As long as it's my home, she's welcome here.

Sissy: She's welcome in my home too.

Marcus: Get out.

Jane: I'm sorry. I never meant to cause trouble. Come on, Mary. *(Jane and Mary exit.)*

Bonnie: How come you're being so mean to Jane and Mary?

Butch: You're just like the innkeeper in the first Christmas.

Marcus: What do you mean?

Butch: Bonnie read me the story last night. Sissy told us the innkeeper had no room for Jesus. You have no room for Jesus either.

Sissy: Butch is right. If you knew Jesus, you'd never have turned Jane and Mary away.

Bonnie: The shepherds knew Jesus was important. I know Jesus is important too.

Sissy: God loves us. Jane told us that. I'm going out to find her and tell her I made a decision last night. I believe in Jesus, just like Matthew. *(Sissy throws on her jacket and heads for the door.)*

Butch and Bonnie *(grabbing their coats):* Wait for us! We're coming too. *(Leave hurriedly.)*

Marcus: Wait! You can't go!

Catherine: They'll leave you some day, just like Matthew did, if you don't change your ways.

Marcus: Don't you think I know that? Every day I live in fear that this is the moment Sissy will leave this house and never return. And now it's here.

Catherine: It doesn't have to be this way. Last night I prayed for the first time in years. You ought to try it!

Marcus: That woman is here for less than 24 hours and she's turned everyone against me, even my own mother!

Catherine: That woman has a name! Jane Tyler! She's your daughter-in-law, and you cut her off just like you did Matthew. Don't you realize she and Mary are your only connection to your son! What ails you, Marcus?

Marcus: What makes you think I want any connection to Matthew? Let the past stay buried with my son. I don't want to dredge up all those painful memories.

Catherine: Ha! You've never buried the past! You live there. You certainly don't live in this house with this family. You wear the past like a pair of dark glasses, and it's blinded you to life.

MARCUS: Don't go there, Ma! You've gone too far!

CATHERINE: You think I don't know about the bitterness of your life? It's my life, too, and Jane's and Sissy's and Bonnie's and Butch's and sweet little Mary's. You made a mistake and it ruined your relationship with your oldest child. If you keep holding onto it, if you don't let it go, it's going to ruin your relationship with each of your children. Let it go, Marcus.

MARCUS: It isn't that easy.

CATHERINE: Listen to me! I told you I prayed last night, Marcus. I'm not talking about a little "Now I lay me down to sleep" sweetness and light prayer. I talked with God! It wasn't easy! You're right about that part. It was tears and agony and heartbreak. I was exhausted when I finished pouring out my soul, but for the first time in a long time I feel hopeful. There is hope for this family. Let go of your guilt and self-pity before it eats you up and there's nothing left. Show your children how much you love them, Marcus.

(Sissy, Butch, Bonnie, Jane, and Mary enter quietly.)

MARCUS: It's too late. It won't do any good. I loved Matthew, but I threw him out of this house. I never got the chance to apologize or say good-bye. I'll never have that chance. I'll never forgive myself.

JANE *(steps forward and picks up the present under the tree):* It was a mistake for me to go. I can't do it. I made a promise to God and to Matthew. I won't leave until I tell you what I came here to say. Matthew forgave you. He tried to call and tell you. He tried to write to you but you would never speak to him or listen to him. That's why we were coming here for Christmas. Matthew and I picked out this present for you. He wanted you to have it.

(Jane hands the present to Marcus. Marcus turns it over in his hands but doesn't open it. Mary takes it out of Marcus' hands, opens it to reveal a Bible and gives it back to him. Marcus opens the front cover of the Bible.)

MARCUS: Matthew wrote this, didn't he? I can't read it.

JANE *(takes the Bible and reads):* "To Dad, I have found the best gift of all, the gift of life and love and I want to share it with you. Love,

Matthew." "For God so loved the world that he gave his one and only Son, that whoever believes in him shall not perish but have eternal life" (John 3:16).

MARY: That's God's Christmas present to all of us.

(Marcus remains silent and all eyes are fastened on him. Jane tries to give him the Bible but he refuses to take it.)

BUTCH: Aren't you going to take it, Dad?

(Marcus gives a weary negative shake of the head.)

SISSY: It's still snowing outside, Dad. Jane and Mary can't leave now. The street isn't even plowed. They'll have to stay.
BONNIE: Today is Christmas Eve! They'll have to stay for Christmas.
BUTCH: Can they stay, Dad?
MARCUS: They can stay if they want. I don't care. *(He leaves.)*
BONNIE: This is great! We can sing carols and bake cookies.
BUTCH: And eat cookies!
CATHERINE: Be still, children.
JANE *(looking sad and somber):* Excuse me. *(Jane exits.)*

Scene 7

Marcus' study, a few moments later. Marcus is seated at his desk, head in his hands. Jane enters. Marcus raises his head, grabs a pen and begins to write on the paper in front of him.

MARCUS: I'm busy. I said you and the little girl could stay . . . as long as you like. *(Jane puts the Bible on the corner of the desk.)* I don't want that Bible. You keep it.
JANE *(softly):* I can't. It meant so much to Matthew to give you this. We talked about this moment many times. Can't you find it in your heart to forgive him and accept his gift?
MARCUS: Matthew's dead. Whatever I do, or don't do, at this point doesn't matter. I can't accept Matthew's gift or his beliefs.

26   *No Room*

JANE: You mean you won't! Just like you wouldn't accept Matthew's attempts to apologize over the years. You wouldn't accept his forgiveness or give him yours!

MARCUS: You come in here for one day and think you know everything about this family. You don't! You don't know a thing! I forgave Matthew the day I learned of his death, but I will not forgive a God who would do this to me. Your God, Matthew's God, He has no place in my life.

JANE: I know. I'm . . .

MARCUS *(angrily cuts her off):* Don't preach to me! You give me one good reason why I should listen, why I should want any part of a God who would murder my son. Why did Matthew have to die?

JANE: I don't know, I . . .

MARCUS: Exactly. You don't know! Your faith is nothing. A placebo to make you feel better, that's all!

JANE: No, it's not!

MARCUS: Prove it! Give me a reason! Matthew was a good boy, one in a million, and he's dead. Yet your God allows axe murderers and child molesters to walk around free! I demand to know why!

JANE: God has a perfect plan and Matthew was in His plan. There's a good reason for everything that happens in our lives. Sometimes it's hard to understand and see God's reason at the time they happen, but later on, I'll see and I'll understand.

MARCUS: Don't give me that hindsight 20/20 line. It's religious drivel. I've heard it all before. You're no different. Your faith is worthless. I've heard enough. *(Marcus hands her the Bible.)* Close the door when you leave.

JANE *(holds the Bible close to her heart for a moment, struggling for the right words, then her body tenses and she takes a step forward and places the Bible on the desk squarely in front of Marcus):* You think I don't know how you feel? Matthew was my only family until Mary came along. I've lost my family. You've had yours all along and you've turned your back on it and thrown it away. You say you want a reason why Matthew is gone! I'll give you a reason! For as long as I've know Matthew, he wanted to get back together with you and make things right. He was desperate to see his brother and sisters, to talk with his grandmother, to keep his promise to teach Sissy how to drive a stick shift. You wouldn't allow him to come back. You robbed him of the love he wanted to share with his family—with you! It was you who killed your son years ago, not God. You took him away from everything he loved. You treated him as if he were dead. Well, you finally got what you wanted. Now he is dead and that's your wake-up call from God.

(Jane cuts herself off and trembles in the thick silence. Marcus gets up, turns away, and stares out the window. Jane creeps over, reaches out her hand and places it on his shoulder; but when Marcus turns his flinty face to hers, she pulls it back.)

JANE: I'm sorry. I had no right to speak to you like that. I know God cares about this family. I was wrong to place my human interpretation on God's actions for your life. That's between you and God.

(Marcus turns away without a word and stomps out of the study. Jane stands alone, heartbroken.)

Scene 8

Christmas morning, all the family except Marcus, is gathered around the cardboard tree. Butch, Bonnie, and Mary are laughing and talking. Catherine is seated at Jane's side. Marcus enters with shopping bags, and underneath them all, Matthew's Bible. Catherine takes Jane's hand and holds it warmly and securely in her own. Sissy greets her father and Marcus hands her a bag, then begins distributing the others to Butch, Bonnie, and finally Catherine.

MARCUS: Merry Christmas, Ma.
CATHERINE: Merry Christmas yourself. Where have you been, Marcus? We've all been waiting for you.

(Butch opens his bag and pulls out a present wrapped in the comics from the newspaper.)

BUTCH: Dad, you wrapped your Christmas presents? What gives?

(Bonnie and Sissy look in their bags and find similarly wrapped gifts. Mary watches wide-eyed.)

BONNIE: Yeah, Dad. What's going on?

MARCUS *(a trifle gruffly):* You don't need to make a big deal out of it. Just open them already.

BUTCH *(hands one of his gifts to Mary, then brings another to Jane, he grins and laughs):* Merry Christmas! I don't know what it is but I hope you like it.

JANE: But Butch, these are your gifts.

BUTCH *(shrugs and smiles):* I wanted to get you and Mary something special but I didn't have a chance because of the storm. *(He shrugs sheepishly.)* And I didn't have any money either. *(He flops down beside Mary.)* Open it, Mary, I want to see what you got.

(Mary looks at her mother; then, at Jane's nod, begins to tear open the package.)

MARCUS: Butch, that present was for you.

CATHERINE: Leave the boy alone, Marcus. I'm proud of you, Butch. Right at this moment, you remind me so much of your older brother, Matthew. Don't you think so, Sissy?

SISSY: Yes, Gram. He does. *(Sissy gives her younger brother a hug.)*

BUTCH *(shrugs it off but smiles as he complains):* Hey, what was that for?

SISSY: Just because . . .

(Marcus clears his throat too loudly and all eyes turn to him. In his hand he carries the Bible. He puts a tentative hand on Jane's shoulder.)

CATHERINE: Marcus, please, it's Christmas. Don't ruin it for the children.

MARCUS *(holds up his hands in a placating gesture):* It's okay, Ma, relax. Butch giving away his presents? I never thought I'd see the day. If miracles can happen with him, maybe this family's not as far gone as you thought. *(He turns somber and faces Jane.)* Jane, I was going to give you this Bible again. *(Jane opens her mouth to protest* *but a self-deprecating laugh from Marcus silences her.)* I said, I was, but I have a feeling you'd find a way to get it back to me. I tried to convince myself this morning that you and Mary should have it; that you needed it to keep Matthew close. It was a part of Matthew that belonged to you, not me. I never got the chance . . . *(He pauses, searching for words and a handle on his emotions.)* I never allowed myself the opportunity to know the man that Matthew was.

JANE *(reaches out and clasps Marcus' hands):* He was a good man.

MARCUS: I'm just beginning to discover that for myself. If you don't mind, I'd like to keep this.

JANE: Matthew would like that.

MARCUS: It may sound crazy, but I can almost hear his voice when I read it.

CATHERINE *(rises from her seat and puts her arm around Marcus):* It's the sanest thing I've heard from you in ages.

MARCUS: I think I understand what you were trying to tell me yesterday, Jane, but I have a long way to go. I want to start over. I apologize. I'm sorry I hurt you. *(Jane gives him a hug.)* I can see why Matthew chose you to be a part of his family. I hope you'll give me, give us, another chance. Will you stay Jane? I've wasted so much time. I'd really like to get to know my new daughter and my first granddaughter. I'd like to learn about Matthew and his faith. I need all of it.

(All the family gathers around Marcus, Jane and Catherine. Marcus picks up Mary.)

SISSY: You will stay, won't you, Jane?

JANE: Yes, you're our family now. That's the finest Christmas present Mary and I could imagine. Thank you, Marcus.

MARCUS: Merry Christmas, Jane. Merry Christmas Mary.

MARY: Are you my grandpa now?

MARCUS: Yes. Yes, I am. Now and forever.

MARY: Merry Christmas, Grandpa.

(Group hug.)

Missing Baby Jesus

Paula Reed

In our rush to celebrate Christmas, we must not forget what Christmas is really about.

Characters:
MOM, Maggie
DAD, Harold
GRANDMA, Mother Carlisle
ALLYSON, daughter
REBECCA, daughter

Setting and Props: Living room scene, bare Christmas tree, phone, two or three boxes labeled "decorations," garland, nativity scene, blueprint, strand of lights

As scene opens, Mom enters with two children. Mom is obviously in a panic with so many things to do. The children are carrying boxes of decorations.

MOM: Allyson, you start hanging the garland and Rebecca, you can put out the nativity scene. Hurry now girls, we have a lot to do!

(Allyson begins pulling garland out of one of the boxes and hanging it on the tree. Rebecca begins setting out the nativity scene.)

MOM: Girls, where's Daddy? *(Impatient.)* I have a list for him too!
ALLYSON: I think he's in the basement looking for the box of outdoor lights.

(At this point a loud crash is heard offstage.)

MOM: What on earth was that?
REBECCA: I think it was Daddy.
MOM *(running to door and yelling downstairs):* Harold! Harold! What's going on down there?

(Dad walks in, hair disheveled and lights all over him. Girls run over to him to see if he's okay. Mom is standing there looking a little perturbed.)

MOM: Harold, is this your way of getting out of putting up the decorations?

DAD: Sure, Maggie. I purposely dropped the box of lights on my head so maybe, just maybe, I'd get a concussion and sleep through Christmas! *(Thoughtfully.)* Hey, that's not a bad idea.

MOM *(glaring at Dad):* Funny, Harold, real funny.

REBECCA *(worried):* Mommy! Daddy could be hurt!

DAD *(scooping Rebecca up in his arms):* No, Becca, I'm not hurt. Just a few lights short of a strand is all. *(Girls laugh.)* Now, you go on and help your Mommy.

REBECCA: But, Daddy, I . . .

DAD: Rebecca, Mommy needs all our help right now. So go on and do your job. *(Gives Rebecca a playful nudge and she goes back to the nativity scene. It is obvious she is missing something as she searches through papers in box.)*

MOM: Now, Harold, about those outdoor decorations. Last night when I couldn't sleep because I couldn't stop thinking about all there is to do, I drew up a plan for the decorations this year. Look! *(Pulls out a big blueprint and Dad about falls over in disbelief.)*

DAD *(incredulous):* Maggie! What on earth is this? What happened to a few strands of lights on a couple of evergreens? Are we putting lights on the entire city?

REBECCA *(comes over and tugs on Mom's shirt):* Mommy, we're missing . . .

MOM *(cutting her off):* Not now, Rebecca. I'm trying to organize your Daddy—go on now and finish the nativity scene.

REBECCA: But Mom . . .

MOM: Now, Rebecca!

(Rebecca goes and gets Allyson and they go to the nativity scene.)

MOM *(turning back to Dad):* Now, Harold, last year the Benders across the street won the city's outdoor Christmas decorating contest and I haven't heard the end of it from Mrs. Bender. Gloat,

gloat, gloat—that's all she did for weeks! Why she even went so far as to give me suggestions of how to help make our pathetic outdoor decorations better! This should show her and everyone else.

DAD: Maggie, Honey, isn't this overkill? And since when did Christmas become a contest about decorating? I'll have to work double shifts just to pay the electric bill for this!

MOM *(rolls her eyes at him):* Oh, Harold, stop exaggerating. I figure it'll only take 4,000 lights to beat the Benders this year.

DAD *(incredulous):* Only 4,000 lights? Margaret, that's more watts than we are worth. That's enough—I'm pulling the plug on this idea.

(Girls laugh again at his joke.)

MOM *(angrily closes the blueprint):* Fine, Harold. I'll just string the lights myself.

ALLYSON *(going over to Mom and trying to get her attention):* Mom, we're missing . . .

MOM: Allyson! Not now! Look—you haven't even finished the garland. Am I to do everything myself? Now, please go and don't bother me until you're finished.

DAD *(trying to quiet his wife):* Maggie! Calm down. Christmas is still a whole week away. We've got plenty of time. What else is there to do?

MOM: What else? *(Louder this time.)* What else? Here, take your pick. *(Pulls out several lists.)* There's the shopping, the wrapping, the menu planning, the cooking, the cleaning, oh, and don't forget the Christmas Eve caroling party needs to be organized.

ALLYSON AND REBECCA *(running over to Mom and Dad squealing):* Christmas caroling! We love to go caroling.

DAD *(getting caught up in their excitement grabs the girls and twirls them around):* Hey, Girls, do you know what Christmas Eve would be without caroling?

ALLYSON AND REBECCA *(laughing):* No, Daddy, what?

DAD: A silent night! *(Everyone laughs but Mom who is standing there looking frustrated.)*

MOM: Everybody loves a wise guy. *(Throws hands up in the air.)* Could we get something done around here before Christmas?

DAD *(goes over to Mom and puts an arm around her):* Come on Honey. Lighten up. No pun intended! Aren't we missing a little something here? *(Hamming it up.)* Like joy and glad tidings, peace on earth?

REBECCA *(excited, jumps in between them, interrupting):* I've been trying to tell you. We're missing . . .

MOM *(interrupting again):* Joy, glad tidings, and peace on earth? It's Christmas. Who's got time for all that when there's so much to do? I'll be at peace when all this is done.

(The girls see Grandma entering the room and run to her excited and yell "Grandma.")

DAD: Mom! You're here early.

MOM *(frantically searching through her lists and talking to herself):* Mother Carlisle—she's not on my list until Tuesday and this is Saturday. Now I'm three days behind.

GRANDMA: I thought I'd come down early and see if you could use some help. I hope that's okay.

DAD: Of course, Mom. Believe me, we could use all the help we can get. *(Gets glaring look from Maggie.)* Isn't this a nice surprise, Honey?

MOM *(forcing a smile and going over to Grandma):* It's certainly a surprise, Mother Carlisle, and we are glad you're here. Wouldn't you like to go rest a bit after your trip?

GRANDMA: Rest? I get plenty of that. Why don't you give me one of your lists, dear, and I'll start working on it.

MOM *(hurriedly crams lists into pockets):* Lists? What lists? *(Grandma keeps looking at her and she sheepishly hands one over to her.)* Well, okay, there are probably a few things I could use some help with.

GRANDMA: Honey, are you sure you wouldn't like to go and rest a bit? You seem a little tense.

MOM: Tense? I'm not tense!

(Rebecca gets up and tugs on Grandma who bends over to hear her as she whispers in her ear. Grandma follows her over to the nativity scene where the rest of the family has gathered. Phone rings.)

MOM *(answering phone gruffly):* Hello? Yes, this is the Carlisle's. No, I'm not willing to donate any more money to your organization. What? Yes, I know it's Christmas and everybody and their brother has a charity all of a sudden! *(Louder.)* What do you mean, "Where's my Christmas spirit?" Where's yours? Are you going to help us pay for our Christmas bills when they start rolling in? Are you willing to help me cook, clean, shop, decorate . . . hello? Hello? *(Slams phone down and turning sees family staring at her in disbelief.)*

DAD *(quietly):* Honey, we're missing something here.

MOM *(ruffled):* What could we possibly be missing? I have everything right here on my lists!

ALLYSON: Mom, please listen.

REBECCA *(almost crying):* Mommy, we're missing baby Jesus.

MOM *(starts to search frantically through the papers in the box):* Missing baby Jesus? That can't be—it has to be here. I know he was here last year. Oh, I don't have time go looking for baby Jesus. And what's Christmas without a baby Jesus?

(Family continues to watch her quietly. Mom soon realizes what she has said and what she has been doing.)

MOM *(quietly and softly):* Missing baby Jesus?

(Allyson in the meantime has gone over to another box and finding baby Jesus brings it to Mom.)

ALLYSON: Look, Mom, he's not missing. He was just misplaced. It's OK.

MOM: No, Allyson, it's not OK. I was wrong, very wrong. I misplaced Jesus here *(Points to heart.)* where it matters most. *(Looks at family.)* I'm very sorry. *(Turns to Rebecca.)* Rebecca, would you like to finish the nativity scene now?

REBECCA *(placing the baby Jesus in the nativity scene):* There Mommy. Jesus is right where He belongs.

MOM: Yes, Becca. He certainly is.

(Lights dim and the family exits.)

The Carpenter's Cradle
Paula Reed

A Christmas Eve service

Cast:
JOSEPH
MOTHER, Joseph's mother
NARRATOR

Staging: Set should resemble a carpenter's shop in biblical times. Various pieces of wood are lying around, worktable has the makings of a cradle on it. Two stools are in workroom—one behind table, one next to table. A couple of lanterns are lit to give light.

Scripture quotations are from the *Holy Bible, New International Version.*

The scene opens on the carpenter's shop with Joseph working on the finishing touches of a baby cradle. Mother enters the workroom.

MOTHER: Ahh, Joseph. What a beautiful piece you are working on!
JOSEPH: Hello, Mother. *(He goes over to mother and embraces her and offers her a seat next to the worktable.)* You speak as a true mother, praising before the work is finished.
MOTHER *(smiling at Joseph):* But it is true. I can already see the fine craftsmanship and I know it will be beautiful. You have learned the trade well, Joseph.
JOSEPH: All that I have learned I owe to my father. He was a great carpenter and teacher.
MOTHER: My son speaks the truth, and your father would be proud.

(A few seconds pass as the mother watches the son work. Presently she gives a deep sigh and slight shake of her head.)

JOSEPH: What is it, Mother? I hear a volume of unspoken words in your sighing.

MOTHER: Dare I speak? I am but a poor, Jewish woman, the wife of a simple carpenter. Who am I to question the events leading up to the fashioning of this cradle?

JOSEPH *(stops working for a moment):* Please, tell me what it is that troubles you so?

MOTHER: Mary, she is such a sweet child and yet, her story, her "vision" as she says, seems more than my feeble mind can take in.

JOSEPH: I know, Mother. It is beyond my understanding as well and at first I chose not to believe it. My head pounded with the knowledge that my beloved Mary was going to have a child . . . a child I knew wasn't mine! But my heart . . . my heart pounded with the knowledge that Mary would never have betrayed me so!

MOTHER *(speaking softly and tenderly, touches Joseph):* My dear Joseph, you have always been filled with kindness, a righteous man you are! *(Pause.)* But it might be said that kindness could be used to cover another's shame.

JOSEPH *(ponders his words for a moment):* I know that your words reflect the wisdom that comes from a life that has lived long and seen much. And the truth is I felt much the same upon hearing the news. I had decided to divorce Mary quietly at first to spare her from further shame and embarrassment. *(Pauses and then speaks quietly.)* This hurt me deeply, as I do love her so. But when the angel spoke to me and told me that Mary's story was true, my heart rejoiced with the news! We are to be a family!

MOTHER *(smiling at Joseph):* I rejoice with you, my son. And yet . . . can you be sure?

JOSEPH *(quietly, with conviction):* Yes, of this I am sure—Jehovah has spoken and His words are true! Must I do any less than choose to believe and act on that truth?

MOTHER: Of course not, my child. I am blessed to have a son with such faith! And I am ashamed to have questioned the messenger sent from Jehovah himself. Please, tell me again the words the angel spoke to you.

JOSEPH: I never tire of telling the story, Mother. It still fills me with wonder. The angel appeared to me in a dream and said: "Do not be afraid to take Mary home as your wife, because what is conceived in her is from the Holy Spirit. She will give birth to a son, and you are to give him the name Jesus, because he will save his people from their sins" (Matthew 1:20, 21).

MOTHER: It is an amazing vision, Joseph. But I must admit I still don't understand it all. The prophets of old spoke of such a time as this. Forgive me for speaking so boldly, but I had envisioned something bigger than a . . . a carpenter's cradle.

JOSEPH: I would not be truthful if I said I understood it all. How can I, a mere man, understand the ways of the God of our fathers, Abraham, Isaac, and Jacob? I know many call me a fool for my beliefs—many have said that I am weak for putting my faith in a vision and for my belief in something I don't fully understand. Some of our own people shun Mary and me in the marketplace and hurl their insults behind our backs. But if I'm a fool, at least I am Jehovah's fool, and where I am weak, I pray He will be strong!

MOTHER: My son speaks with such honor and strength! May God's favor always shine upon you.

JOSEPH: I seek His favor as well as His guidance in the days and weeks to come. I worry for Mary and me, but especially for the Child who is yet to come. What is to become of Him?

MOTHER: We would do well to remember what Isaiah said in the Scripture, that God's ways are not our ways or His thoughts our thoughts. We only see a small part, Joseph—that which is here and now. To think beyond that tires the body as well as the soul.

(Joseph appears troubled as he continues to work on the cradle. A few seconds pass before his mother speaks to him.)

MOTHER *(speaking softly)*: What is it, Joseph?

JOSEPH: I know you speak the truth, Mother. But I am just Joseph, the son of a carpenter. Why would God choose me for this?

MOTHER: Perhaps it is your humble spirit that He seeks. Or perhaps it is simply the fact that you believe.

JOSEPH: Perhaps. All I know is that I'm about to be a father and in such a way that is still a mystery to me. And soon this cradle will be filled and with a child sent from God! I am frightened of the responsibility, Mother. A cradle I can shape with wood and nails, but to shape the child within the cradle . . . ahhh, that is a different thing indeed!

MOTHER: It is an honorable thing to be humble enough to fear the responsibility of bringing up a child. But God has chosen you and Mary for this. We must believe that He will also supply the strength and wisdom needed for such a task.

JOSEPH: I feel we will need much in the days yet to come. *(A few more seconds pass as he continues to ponder all this and then stops working for this next dialogue. He builds with emotion as he speaks.)* I can't help but wonder though; how will this child, a mere child, save our people? Will He be a great leader of people and gather an army to crush our enemies? Will He be mighty in battle as our ancestor King David? Will this child named Jesus become a powerful king whose empire will devour those who now oppose us? Oh, how long we have waited for the Messiah to redeem us!

MOTHER: Oh, Joseph—hearing you speak fills this tired, old woman with fresh hope! It is true our people have lived with the expectation that our Redeemer would come and deliver us. Many who have gone before us spoke of the hope and dreamed of this day. We have not always agreed how this mystery will be fulfilled and who would have imagined it would be found in a simple carpenter's cradle?

(Both pause and reflect on the words that have just been spoken. At this point both are looking at the cradle.)

JOSEPH: I can't help but wonder about this Child who is to be my son. Will our people accept Him as the promised One? Will His life be an easier one than the one we have known? What will become of Him beyond the cradle?

(Lights dim on center stage and Joseph and his mother exit as song of your choice is played. Narrator makes his way to the front at the end of the song.)

NARRATOR: We can only speculate as to what Mary and Joseph felt as they awaited the miraculous birth of the Son of God. We can be sure there was a certain fear, a certain wonder, and an overwhelming sense of awe as they beheld His birth on that starry, silent night.

The long awaited Messiah quietly entered our world and along with Him came the birth of our salvation. Confusion over the baby in the simple manger caused many to see only the swaddling clothes and not the Savior who lay within. The long-awaited Messiah did not bring the mighty armies or fight the glorious battles envisioned by many because His kingdom was not of this world. For the battles that ensued over His coming were fought not on a battlefield, but in the hearts and souls of mankind. And it is a war for our souls that still rages on. Satan would have us ignore the true reason for this season and focus instead on the secular trappings of this holiday. But the truth remains that Jesus Christ, our Messiah and King of kings shed His royal robes, stepped from His heavenly throne, and in true humility, proved His obedience through His birth and again through His death. For beyond the cradle was the cross and beyond the cross was our redemption. Honoring His birth rekindles our hope and remembering His supreme sacrifice on the cross rekindles our faith. We cannot begin to explain or comprehend the passion God feels for each one of us, but may we embrace His incredible love that reaches through all time and space and covers us with His grace and mercy. As we prayerfully observe and partake of Communion on this Christmas Eve, may we experience anew the hope that comes from knowing Christ and may we humble ourselves at His feet and acknowledge Him as Lord and Savior.

COMMUNION

CANDLELIGHT SERVICE

SONG: "Silent Night" *(Is sung as candles are lit.)*

CLOSING PRAYER

The Shepherds' Wives

V. Louise Cunningham

Characters:
SARAH
TERAH, young wife
ELIZABETH, older woman
MARY
DEBBIE
MARCIE
TAMERA, last minute shopper

Setting: Contemporary scene with a table and chairs, and two Bible-time scenes, one of a kitchen scene and the other a stable. Could use a split stage.

Props: Table, coffeepot, mugs, doll, kettle, blankets, baby clothes

Scene 1

Scene opens on a contemporary setting with three women sitting around a table drinking coffee.

DEBBIE: Hard to believe that Christmas is just around the corner. Do you have everything ready?

TAMERA: Are you kidding. I'm the one who does her shopping on December 24.

MARCIE: I'm finished with everything so I can sit back and enjoy the holidays.

DEBBIE: There always has to be one.

TAMERA: Why couldn't it be me?

MARCIE: Because you have to plan ahead and work on things all year.

TAMERA: I remember my grandmother did that. She hid things in shopping bags all around the house and when the holidays came, she couldn't find the things she had bought.

DEBBIE: At least Mary didn't have to worry about Christmas.

TAMERA: And if you remember, the wise men didn't get there until Jesus was a child. And you think I'm behind on my shopping.

MARCIE: Have you ever thought about the shepherds' wives?

DEBBIE: Do you think the shepherds were married?

TAMERA: Why wouldn't they be? Shepherding would be a job like any other.

MARCIE: I wonder if they sat around like we are now, having a cup of whatever they drank.

Scene 2

A Bible-time scene with Elizabeth sitting at the table.

SARAH *(knocking on door):* Hi, it's just me.

ELIZABETH *(opening door):* Come in. I wondered how long it would be before somebody came to my door.

SARAH: Then your husband told you the same story mine did?

ELIZABETH: I can't say for sure until we compare, but probably.

SARAH: I've never seen Joel so excited. He told me about seeing angels in the sky who told Joel and the other shepherds the Messiah was born. Then the shepherds went to Bethlehem and disturbed some poor couple in a stable to see their baby.

ELIZABETH: Sounds like about the same thing I heard.

SARAH: Do you think there is any truth to it?

(A knock is heard.)

ELIZABETH: It has to be Terah. *(Opens the door.)* Come in Terah. I was just telling Sarah it had to be you.

TERAH: Then your husbands told you the same story?

SARAH: We were just comparing notes. Did Timothy tell you that the sky opened up and it was full of angels?

TERAH: Something like that. Then these beings said the shepherds were to go and find a baby wrapped in swaddling clothes lying in a manger. Doesn't that beat all?

ELIZABETH: You don't think there is truth in that? I wouldn't think that all of the shepherds would dream the same thing on one night.

Sarah: They did find a baby.

Terah: Yes, but the Messiah wouldn't be born in a stable!

Elizabeth: Why couldn't He be?

Terah: I think the Messiah would be born in a palace or at least in the home of nobility, not in a dirty stable.

Elizabeth: The Messiah is coming for all people. Do you think we would be welcomed into a fancy house to see the Messiah?

Terah: No, but the Son of God deserves better than to be born in a stable.

Elizabeth: We have a wonderful God and He does work in mysterious ways.

Sarah: What do you think we should do?

Terah: About what?

Sarah: Do you think we dare go and see the Messiah?

Terah: If they are in a stable, they could use some food or blankets. We could take something to them? Do you think that would be all right, Elizabeth?

Elizabeth: I think that would be a good idea. I have some soup simmering. We could take some of that over.

Terah: I have some new baby clothes I could take.

Elizabeth: Are you sure you want to do that?

Terah: It's all right. By the time I get pregnant again I'll have time to make some more baby things. If He really is the Messiah I would be honored if the mother would accept them.

Sarah: I'll see what I have. Let's meet back here around lunchtime.

Terah: Sounds good to me.

Elizabeth: I'll just add a few more vegetables to the soup and I'll be ready in a few minutes. I wonder if the Messiah has really come. I remember when I was a little girl playing with other girls and we'd take turns being the mother of the Messiah. Then when I wasn't chosen I hoped one of our girls would be. I remember hearing that the Messiah was to be born of a virgin. There were a lot of other prophecies, but now my mind goes blank on what they were. It seems like there was one that said where He would be born.

Scene 3

The three women are standing outside the stable. Mary and the baby are inside.

SARAH: Joel said this is the stable. Now that we're here, I'm kind of afraid.

ELIZABETH: Why? She can't do more than tell us to go and mind our own business. If she does, you can all come over for soup.

TERAH: She'll probably be glad to have some help, since she's a stranger in town.

SARAH: Some people like to be left alone if they aren't feeling well or have just had a baby.

TERAH: Maybe they have found a better place to live and they aren't here anymore.

ELIZABETH: This soup is getting heavy and we won't find out anything if all we do is stand out here yammering. Let's go in.

SARAH: Now that I think of it, isn't it strange to be carrying some soup into a stable. People might think there's a sick cow in there or something. *(Giggles.)*

ELIZABETH: Good morning. Is there anyone here? Hello . . .

MARY: Yes, who is it? I'm over here.

ELIZABETH: We heard you gave birth to a son last night and we thought you might like a little lunch brought in.

MARY: That's very kind of you. My husband, Joseph, had to leave for a few minutes, but I'm sure he'll be back soon.

TERAH: I brought some baby clothes you might be able to use.

MARY: That's very thoughtful of you. I wasn't able to bring much with us. We were hoping we would be back home before the baby came. We had to be here for the census. When we got here all the inns were full and I was in labor. The innkeeper said we could use his stable.

TERAH: What a precious baby. What did you name Him?

MARY: Jesus.

ELIZABETH: Of course, it would be. It means the Lord saves.

MARY: Tell me again how you knew I was here.

SARAH: Our husbands are shepherds and they came home all excited. They said the sky opened up and they saw angels. The angels told

The Shepherds' Wives

them they would find you here with a baby and that He was the Messiah.

MARY: Did you believe them?

TERAH: I would like to believe.

MARY: If you have a few minutes, I'll tell you and you can make your own decision.

ELIZABETH: Are you sure you aren't too tired? We didn't plan on staying very long.

MARY: It won't take very long. I was engaged to Joseph and one night an angel came and told me that I was going to have a baby. I asked how could that be since I had never known a man. The angel replied that the Holy Spirit would come upon me and I would have a child I would call Jesus.

TERAH: Weren't you scared?

MARY: Scared is putting it mildly. I was terrified even though the angel said not to be afraid. When I told Joseph I was pregnant, he was going to divorce me. He didn't understand until an angel came to him.

SARAH: What a relief that must have been.

MARY: It was. I went to visit my cousin Elizabeth, and she was miraculously expecting too. Both she and her husband, Zechariah, are pretty old to be having a baby and an angel spoke to Zechariah in the temple. Because he didn't believe the angel, he was speechless until the baby came.

SARAH: You make it sound so simple. There must have been some difficult times.

MARY: There was the usual tongue wagging when the women in town started counting months and how long Joseph and I had been married.

ELIZABETH: Yes, we women can sometimes be very nasty.

MARY: There were times when I sometimes thought the angel visiting us was a dream and God really didn't talk to me, but last night confirmed again in my mind that this is the Son of God.

SARAH: What was it that reassured you?

MARY: Your husbands coming to see us because angels spoke with them and told them where to find us.

ELIZABETH: That was very strange. Well, Mary, if there isn't anything we can do for you, we will let you rest.

SARAH: Imagine, we saw the Messiah. Thank you, Mary.

Scene 4

This scene is with the three contemporary women sitting at the table.

DEBBIE: You know, in Luke it says that the shepherds told people about the birth and the people who heard it were amazed. I wonder what all those people did after they heard.

MARCIE: I wonder if they believed. After all, you wouldn't think the shepherds would be easy people to fool. They were pretty practical.

TAMERA: Isn't it something that God chose hard-working men to be the first witnesses?

MARCIE: The world wasn't easy for the Jews at that time. There were high taxes, they were under Roman law, and a military state was in control. Add to that Greek philosophy and the strict Jewish religion.

DEBBIE: And into that situation God sent His Son.

MARCIE: The amazing thing to me is that although Jesus was a baby, He was God. God was in a manger.

TAMERA: If Jesus had been born in a palace, the simple people would not have been allowed to see Him.

DEBBIE: We can certainly learn from the shepherds.

TAMERA: What's that?

DEBBIE: To go and tell others the good news. The Savior of the world has come and they will want to know Him personally.

TAMERA: Excellent point and I must be going.

MARCIE: To tell others the good news?

TAMERA: That, of course, and to finish my shopping.

The Shepherds' Wives

The Innkeeper Tells All

Wanda E. Brunstetter

The Innkeeper enters, dressed in a long robe, with a scarf wrapped around his head.

My wife says I'm a mean old man. *(Frowns deeply.)* Can you believe that anyone would call me *(Pointing to self)* mean? She even says that some folks don't like me. Now, I ask you, what's not to like? *(Shrugs his shoulders and extends arms, palms up.)*

After all, I am the innkeeper of my fine little establishment here in Bethlehem. Why I open my doors *(Pulls both hands back as though opening a door)* to weary travelers six days a week. *(Looking very proud and boastful.)* I rest on the seventh day just as the Holy Book says one should do.

(Shrugs his shoulders again.) So, why should anyone think me anything but a kind, righteous man? Perhaps it has something to do with that night when I turned away two weary travelers because I had no room.

(Pointing to self.) But should I be held accountable for that? *(Holding both hands upward.)* All right, so I knew the woman was with child. I could see too that she was extremely tired, as was the man with her. *(Shrugging.)* But could I help it if everyone and his brother were in town to pay their taxes?

I tell you, my rooms were all full! Of course, my wife, Ruth, thought I could have been so gallant as to give up my very own bed. Can you believe anything so preposterous as that? *(Shaking his head slowly.)*

No, I'm a very busy innkeeper, and I need to get my rest. I certainly could not be expected to sleep on the floor or on some tiny little cot so that a taxpayer's wife could have my bed. I'm not selfish you understand, but my own needs must always come first.

Just to prove that I'm really not a mean or harsh man, I did tell the young couple they might take refuge in a nearby stable. It was better than sleeping outside in the cold, wasn't it? *(Holds his hands palms up and begins pacing back and forth.)*

The following day is when things really got bad around here. My wife got the news from someone that the pregnant woman who had been here the night before, had given birth to a son right there in the stable where I had sent them. *(Shaking head.)* I really didn't think she was that close to her delivery time.

Anyway, Ruth was furious with me. She said, "Abner, you are a very mean man to have allowed such a thing. No woman—not even a poor one, should have ever been allowed to deliver a baby among dirty, smelly animals!"

(Shaking head.) You would think I had done it on purpose. *(Pauses and looks thoughtful.)* And then my wife told me something very strange. She said, "Abner, do you know who the baby she delivered is?"

I said, "Well, of course not, dear wife. How should I know?" *(Shrugging.)* I'd never met the man or the woman until that night.

"It is being told among some shepherds that the baby is the Christ Child—the long awaited Messiah," she continued. "Do you know what that means, Husband?"

(He puts one hand to his mouth, then removes it and looks very serious.) If her words were true, then yes, I do know what it means. It means that I really am a mean man. I caused the King of kings to spend the night with lowly creatures in a dark, dreary cave.

(Looking out at audience.) I believe there is a lesson to be learned from my story. What we do for others is as if we are doing to Jesus. I had no idea that I was turning away the mother of Jesus Christ. I had no idea that the Son of God would be born that night in the very stable I had banished them to. *(Points to the audience.)* Are you turning away Jesus too? *(Leaves.)*

The Innkeeper Tells All

Advent Readings

Amy Ridgeway

Five different families can participate in the worship service by reading the Scripture, the devotional, and the prayer before lighting a candle on an Advent wreath. This allows all ages to participate as each family decides who would be responsible for each part.

Scriptures are from the *Holy Bible, New International Version.*

First Sunday

SCRIPTURE: "In the beginning was the Word, and the Word was with God, and the Word was God. He was with God in the beginning. Through him all things were made; without him nothing was made that has been made. In him was life, and that life was the light of men. The light shines in the darkness, but the darkness has not understood it. Yet to all who received him, to those who believed in his name, he gave the right to become children of God—children born not of natural descent, nor of human decision or a husband's will, but born of God" (John 1:1-5, 12, 13).

DEVOTIONAL: Is the Word in the beginning of your Christmas celebration? John tells us that Jesus is the Word, and the Light, and the Life of man. Is He your light? We are here at this time and in this place to be the light of Jesus in a darkening world. We are to be lights showing the way to God, the way to faith, the way to life.

Before any of that can happen, the light of Jesus has to be deep in our own souls, everything that we are and everything that we will be. Our world so desperately needs His light but might not ever understand that light in the darkness. When we receive it, let it fill our lives completely, it might just shine brightly enough to help someone else along on the path to understanding, step by step.

PRAYER: Dear God, we ask that You be with us in our beginnings, that Your Word be in our hearts, and that we let it shine in our lives and in our world this Christmas. Amen.

Second Sunday

SCRIPTURE: "A record of the genealogy of Jesus Christ the son of David, the son of Abraham: . . . Thus there were fourteen generations in all from Abraham to David, fourteen from David to the exile to Babylon, and fourteen from the exile to the Christ" (Matthew 1:1, 17).

DEVOTIONAL: Who says that God doesn't make sense? Sometimes patterns exist that we can't even see until the end is accomplished. Abraham longed for a son, not even suspecting that his son would be the life of all of us. David killed a giant to save his world, not knowing that his Son would change our world completely.

Matthew shows us that Jesus was real: a real son, a real baby, and a real person just as we are.

Our challenge at this time is to be real, just like Jesus. He became one of us to show us how to become one with Him.

Don't let this Christmas go by without a real, authentic celebration of all that Jesus is in our lives. Show His humility and humanity to a world that needs a real Jesus, a real faith, and a real person to help them along their journey of faith.

PRAYER: Dear God, help us to be real this Christmas, to celebrate your gifts of all that we are and guide us on to all that we are able to become when you are the real and authentic center of our souls. Amen.

Third Sunday

SCRIPTURE: "The beginning of the gospel about Jesus Christ, the Son of God. It is written in Isaiah the prophet: 'I will send my messenger ahead of you, who will prepare your way'—'a voice of one calling in the desert,' 'Prepare the way for the Lord, make straight paths for him.' And so John came, baptizing in the desert region and preaching a baptism of repentance for the forgiveness of sins. And this was his message: 'After me will come one more powerful than I, the thongs of whose sandals I am not worthy to stoop down and untie. I baptize you with water, but he will baptize you with the Holy Spirit'" (Mark 1:1-4, 7, 8).

DEVOTIONAL: Have you heard that voice in the wilderness? And did you ever imagine that the wilderness would exist within the very boundaries of our greatest cities? It is impossible to look at our world and not realize that it is indeed a vast and frightening wild place where individuals lie in wait to wreak havoc on our substance and sustenance, our way of life, and indeed our lives.

John the Baptist did not run from his wilderness, he embraced it and proclaimed the advent of Christ. Nor should we live in a spirit of fear and terror. We need to stand together in our wilderness and proclaim that Christ is here for those who seek Him, for those who want to be baptized with His spirit.

PRAYER: Dear God, let us say together this Christmas, "Prepare the way for the Lord, make straight paths for him." And let us follow His path straight to the center of Your love. Amen.

Fourth Sunday

SCRIPTURE: "Many have undertaken to draw up an account of the things that have been fulfilled among us, just as they were handed down to us by those who from the first were eyewitnesses and servants of the word. Therefore, since I myself have carefully investigated everything from the beginning, it seemed good also to me to write an orderly account for you, most excellent Theophilus, so that you may know the certainty of the things you have been taught" (Luke 1:1-4).

DEVOTIONAL: Are you ready for the best gift you could ever hope to receive?

In just a few days, we will be handed a lot of gifts, and we'll most likely match them gift for gift with an equal treasure. We know a lot about giving and receiving. We have an entire industry devoted to that in America. You can find a card for almost any occasion at a card store. And if you go to a craft store, you can find the materials to make a card for anything the card companies overlooked.

But right here in Luke we find the perfect gift, just what we all need underneath the long list of our desires and dreams.

Eyewitnesses to the miracle of Christ, His servants and disciples handed us the story of Jesus. So did Luke, in an orderly and precise way, Luke gives us the miracle of Jesus, the Word of God, the son of David, the One who gives us God's Holy Spirit.

Don't leave this package under the tree just because it has Theophilus's name on it. Take it out today, unwrap the message and make it a part of every gift you give this Christmas. Listen to Luke, read Luke, and then make his gift of Jesus' story a real, authentic part of your Christmas celebrations.

PRAYER: Dear God, we thank You for this astounding, overwhelming, miraculous gift. Help us to make it ours and keep it alive in our hearts this year. Amen.

Christmas Eve Reading

SCRIPTURE: "For to us a child is born, to us a son in given, and the government will be on his shoulders. And he will be called Wonderful Counselor, Mighty God, Everlasting Father, Prince of Peace" (Isaiah 9:6).

DEVOTIONAL: Many years ago on this night in a humble stable, from a simple woman, that child was born. He went on to reorder our world, writing the rules according to God's holy plan. He is indeed a Wonderful Counselor, directing our paths, is indeed a Mighty God filling our hearts and our souls with an unending supply of His undying love. And if we allow Him to, He will grant us peace and joy.

But we can't let Him stay in that stable of long ago. Jesus grew up to teach us how to love, and to give us the ultimate gift of His love on Easter morning. Our faith needs to grow too. Our faith needs to move beyond this church out into our homes, our workplaces, our schools, our community. Our faith needs to live beyond Sunday morning worship and to grow beyond our solitary devotion.

We need to give our world the message of this night, the simple miraculous truth that God's love was born on earth long ago in Bethlehem, withstood the trials of Calvary, and exists for all of us when we reach out and grab on to His grace.

PRAYER: Dear God, in each of our hearts on this holy night, give us once again the miracle of Your Son. Give us grateful hearts that long to know You and make Your Son the center of our lives tonight, and for all of the other nights when we pause to hear His voice. Amen.

Jesus: Hope of the Ages

Karen L. Mechtly

Cast:
Matt, modern man
Elizabeth, woman of Bethlehem
Abigail, woman of Bethlehem
Martha, young woman of Bethlehem
Claudius, Roman soldier
Marcus, Roman soldier
Simon, innkeeper
Jude, tax collector
Thomas, tax collector
Rachel, shepherd girl
Jacob, Rachel's grandfather
Gabriel, angel messenger
Choir of Angels
Mary, mother of Jesus (nonspeaking)
Joseph, Mary's husband (nonspeaking)
Reader
Stage Crew
Sound Crew

Scripture quotations are from the *Holy Bible, New International Version.*

Act 1

Spotlight on as scene opens on a modern apartment with chair, bookcase, TV and boom box. Matt enters and throws his coat on the chair.

Matt: It's not fair!! This has been the worst day of my life. I can't believe I was fired. I thought my computer job was secure. My future was so bright. Now I'm a has-been. I've been downsized. *(Pulls ring box out of his pocket, opens it, and looks at it.)* I guess I will take Megan's Christmas present back. Why would she want to marry me now?

(He walks over to his boom box, muttering all the way about life not being fair and turns the box on. "Good Christian Men, Rejoice" is playing. He quickly snaps it off.)

MATT: I don't want to hear that stuff now. What do I have to rejoice about? *(Starts pacing back and forth.)* There are hundreds of people looking for jobs. It will be impossible for me to find one. Computers are the only things I know about and no one needs those workers now. *(Shakes his head.)* And this is supposed to be the season to rejoice. Not me, I have no hope at all. *(Slumps dejectedly on the chair.)* What am I going to do? *(He sighs.)* Maybe there is something on TV. *(Picks up the TV log.)* "Frosty the Snowman" or "It's a Wonderful Life"? I don't think so. *(Throws TV log down and looks around the room.)* I know; I'll read something. *(Walks to bookcase, looks at a few books, then selects a Bible.)* What do you know? Here's the Bible my mom gave me when I left home. She always preached Jesus to me when she was alive, but I never listened. And I've never opened this Bible. Maybe she was right. Maybe I can find hope here. *(Opens the Bible.)*

(Lights go out. Matt exits and stage crew removes furniture and puts up Bethlehem background, including an inn and well.)

Act 2

Spotlight on.

CHRISTMAS CHOIR: "O Little Town of Bethlehem"

(Lights on. From right side the three women of Bethlehem enter with their water jars and walk across the stage to the well.)

ELIZABETH *(frowning):* My arms still ache from all the work I did yesterday.

ABIGAIL: Mine too. We work so hard for our husbands and yet they do not appreciate all we do. *(Rubs her back.)*

MARTHA: You would think water ran right into our house the way my family uses it.

(All laugh.)

ABIGAIL: Has it been hard for you to learn to care for Benjamin and his children?
MARTHA *(nodding her head):* Oh, yes. I thought it would be wonderful to have a husband and children, but I never realized how hard wives have to work. Every day it is the same thing—carry water, keep the fire going, bake bread, feed the little ones, mend their clothes.
ABIGAIL: Well, you better get used to it. That's what you will be doing for the rest of your life.
ELIZABETH: You are not more than a child yourself. *(Pats Martha's stomach.)* And probably soon you will have a little one of your own.
MARTHA *(trying to smile):* I know little ones are a gift from God, so I would welcome another one to care for. *(Pauses, then says excitedly.)* Perhaps God will choose me to be the mother of the Messiah. My grandfather told me He would be born here in Bethlehem.
ABIGAIL: Ha! You do not believe those old tales about God sending a Savior, do you?
MARTHA *(puzzled):* Of course I do. My grandfather told me about the Messiah every night at bedtime. The holy Scriptures tell how He will come from Heaven and make our lives better. There will be no more hard work . . .
ELIZABETH *(interrupting):* Some of us think the ancient writers made that story up to give the people something to look forward to.
ABIGAIL: Yes, that story was meant to comfort our people during the captivity in Babylon. It was a hard time for them. But it is only a story.
MARTHA: No, it's not just a story! My grandfather said God himself helped the ancient men write the Scriptures. They wrote the truth. They did not make up stories. God *will* send His Messiah.
ELIZABETH: You can look forward to a Messiah if you want to. But I'm not going to waste my time. People have been looking for a Savior for hundreds of years and he has not yet come.

Jesus: Hope of the Ages

ABIGAIL: You will change your mind when you grow older. The holy Scriptures are beautiful to listen to, but they do not apply to us today.

(Elizabeth and Abigail fill their jars in the well and turn to leave.)

ELIZABETH: Dreamer. You will wise up.

(Elizabeth and Abigail leave the way they came.)

MARTHA *(fills her jar from the well then looks up to Heaven):* Oh God, I do believe You will send a Messiah to save us. I am looking forward to that wonderful day.

(Lights out. Martha pushes well to side as she exits.)

Act 3

(Spotlight on.)

CHRISTMAS CHOIR: "Come, Thou Long-Expected Jesus"

(Lights up. Roman soldiers and tax collectors enter stage noisily. They stop in front of an inn.)

MARCUS: It sure is crowded tonight in Bethlehem. I hope we can find a room in an inn.
CLAUDIUS: Let's try this one. Maybe it is not yet filled. *(Knocks on door.)*
SIMON *(opening the door):* Do you need a room, Sir?
CLAUDIUS: Yes we do.
SIMON *(looking at all four):* I am sorry, but tonight I can only accommodate two more travelers. As long as I have had this inn I have never had so many people knock on my door in one evening.
MARCUS *(to tax collectors as he motions them on):* You men move on and find rooms for yourselves. Claudius and I will stay here.

JUDE: Why you? We are just as important as you in this registering and taxing process. And besides, we are Jews. You are Romans. Move aside and let us go in.

MARCUS: I will not. You might be Jews, but we know the people hate you as much as they hate us. Now, go.

THOMAS *(folds his arms and says defiantly):* We are not moving. There might not be another room available tonight. As the innkeeper has said, this town is full of travelers tonight.

CLAUDIUS *(sneering):* Maybe you will have to sleep on the ground. Of course you are too *soft* to be able to do that.

THOMAS: You miserable Roman. *(He lunges toward Claudius.)*

CLAUDIUS *(draws his sword and puts it on Thomas' chest):* Get out of here, you scum, or you will not see the sun rise tomorrow.

JUDE *(pulls Thomas away):* Thomas, do not be foolish. We can find another inn. You cannot fight a Roman soldier and win.

(Jude and Thomas walk a few paces away.)

CLAUDIUS *(laughs wickedly):* I knew they would see it my way.

MARCUS *(to Innkeeper):* Now, about that room . . .

(Claudius puts sword to Simon's chest.)

MARCUS: It better be the best room you have and the charges better be fair.

(Claudius puts sword away.)

SIMON *(shaking):* Y-y-yes, Sir. Right this way.

(Simon, Claudius, and Marcus walk through inn door.)

JUDE: Thomas, what were you thinking? You could have been killed.

THOMAS: I know. But it angers me that the Romans have taken over our land. Even though I am working for Rome, I cannot stand the Romans.

JUDE: I agree. But what can we do?

Jesus: Hope of the Ages

THOMAS: We can look for the promised Messiah. He will be a mighty soldier. When He comes, we will have victory over the Romans.

JUDE: Do you really think God cares about us any more? He has allowed our country to be taken over by foreigners. We are no longer free. We are all scared.

THOMAS: He does care for us. We are His chosen people and He will rescue us. I know He will.

(Lights out. Thomas and Jude leave. Stage crew replaces Bethlehem scenery with hillside scenery, can include a small fake fire.)

Act 4

Spotlight on.

CHRISTMAS CHOIR: "While Shepherds Watched Their Flocks"

(Lights on. Shepherd girl Rachel, a stuffed lamb by her side, and her grandfather, Jacob, are sitting around a small fire. Sheep baa in the background.)

JACOB: Rachel, look at the night sky. The stars are brighter than I have ever seen them before.

RACHEL: They are beautiful tonight, Grandfather. *(She sighs.)*

JACOB: Is something bothering you, my granddaughter?

(Rachel nods her head.)

JACOB: You can tell me about it.

RACHEL: When I went into Bethlehem today to get some cheese and bread from home, a group of boys laughed at me. They made fun of my old cloak and they said I smelled bad, like sheep.

JACOB: People have always made fun of us shepherds, even though we do an important job by guarding the sheep.

RACHEL: They chased me all the way home. They were going to throw stones at me, but I ducked inside the door just in time.

JACOB: Next time they start to tease you, remind them our great King David was a shepherd boy and our patriarch Isaac and Jacob had wives who were shepherd girls, just like you.

RACHEL: I was too scared to say anything. *(Pause.)* Grandfather, please tell me about the Messiah again.

JACOB: Of course, Rachel. Our holy Scriptures tell us that God will send His Son. He will be called Wonderful Counselor, Mighty God, Everlasting Father and the Prince of Peace. He will reign on David's throne.

RACHEL: Does that mean the Messiah will like shepherds, Grandfather?

JACOB: Oh, yes! The Messiah will love all the people of the earth, rich or poor—important or not. In fact, our Scriptures say the Messiah will care for His people as a shepherd cares for his sheep.

RACHEL *(picks up little stuffed lamb):* That's comforting. *(Pause.)* Do you think God will send the Messiah while we are alive?

JACOB: I hope so, but I do not know. I have been looking for him my whole lifetime. Now I am getting old and . . .

(Gabriel enters with spotlight on him. Lights out. Jacob and Rachel fall prostrate on the ground.)

GABRIEL: "Do not be afraid. I bring you good news of great joy that will be for all the people. Today in the town of David a Savior has been born to you; he is Christ the Lord. This will be a sign to you: You will find a baby wrapped in cloths and lying in a manger" (Luke 2:10-12).

(Spotlight on.)

ANGEL CHOIR: "Angels We Have Heard on High"

(Angels exit. Spotlight goes off. Lights back on.)

RACHEL: Were those real angels, Grandfather, or was I dreaming?

JACOB: They were real. Imagine, God sent His angels to announce the Messiah's birth to poor shepherds.

RACHEL: Let us hurry to Bethlehem and find Him.

Jesus: Hope of the Ages

(Jacob and Rachel rush off. Lights off. Mary, Joseph, and manger are set up on center stage.)

Act 5

Spotlight on.

CHRISTMAS CHOIR: "Adoration" and "O Come, All Ye Faithful"

(Lights on manger scene. Jacob and Rachel rush in.)

JACOB: Praise God! I am blessed to see the Messiah with my own eyes.
RACHEL: Praise God! The Prince of Peace has come.

(They kneel at the manger.)

READER: "But you, Bethlehem Ephrathah, though you are small among the clans of Judah, out of you will come for me one who will be ruler over Israel, whose origins are from of old, from ancient times. He will stand and shepherd his flock in the strength of the Lord, in the majesty of the name of the Lord his God. And they will live securely, for then his greatness will reach to the ends of the earth. And he will be their peace" (Micah 5:2, 4, 5).

THOMAS *(entering):* Praise God! I knew He would not forget His people. *(He kneels at the manger.)*

READER: "'The days are coming,' declares the Lord, 'when I will fulfill the gracious promise I made to the house of Israel and to the house of Judah. In those days and at that time I will make a right-eous Branch sprout from David's line; he will do what is just and right in the land. In those days Judah will be saved and Jerusalem will live in safety. This is the name by which it will be called: The Lord Our Righteousness'" (Jeremiah 33:14-16).

MARTHA: Praise God! I knew it was true. God has sent a Savior. *(She kneels at the manger.)*

READER: "'She will give birth to a son, and you are to give him the name Jesus, because he will save his people from their sins.' All this took place to fulfill what the Lord had said through the prophet: 'The virgin will be with child and will give birth to a son, and they will call him Immanuel'—which means, 'God with us'" (Matthew 1:21-23).

MATT: Praise God! He gives us hope by sending us His Son. *(He kneels at the manger.)*

READER: "Here is my servant, whom I uphold, my chosen one in whom I delight; I will put my Spirit on him and he will bring justice to the nations. In faithfulness he will bring forth justice; he will not falter or be discouraged till he establishes justice on earth. In his law the islands will put their hope" (Isaiah 42:1, 3, 4).

CONGREGATION OR CHOIR: "Joy to the World!"

Jesus: Hope of the Ages

Turkey, Potatoes, and Peas

Carolyn R. Scheidies

Characters: Three groups: Group 1—medium voices; Group 2—low voices; Group 3—high voices

Scriptures are from the *Holy Bible, New International Version.*

GROUP 1: "In that day you will say:
GROUP 2: "Give thanks to the LORD, call on his name; *(Arms up.)*
GROUPS 1 & 3: "Make known among the nations what he has done, *(Arms wide.)*
ALL: "And proclaim that his name is exalted" (Isaiah 12:4). *(Hands around mouth as in megaphone.)*

SONG: "Now Thank We All Our God" *(Verse 1: Solo; Verse 3: All)*

GROUP 1: Thanksgivings come and Thanksgivings go, *(Shrug.)*
ALL: We smile and laugh while gobbling turkey, potatoes, and peas. *(Mimic eating.)*
GROUP 3: Through it all we often forget, *(Tap head.)*
GROUP 2: To thank the one who provided the feast. *(Fold hands.)* "Let them give thanks to the Lord for his unfailing love *(Draw heart in the air.)*
GROUP 1: "And his wonderful deeds for men" (Psalm 107:8). *(Arms wide.)*
GROUP 3: "For he satisfies the thirsty *(Mimic drinking.)*
ALL: "And fills the hungry with good things" (Psalm 107:9). *(Rub stomach.)*
GROUP 3: It's Jesus who provides food and more,
GROUPS 1 & 2: He provides all we hold dear. *(Hug arms to chest.)*
GROUP 2: One day of the year is surely not enough, *(Shake head.)*
GROUP 3: To thank Him who takes away our fear. *(Show fear, point up and smile.)*

LOW SOLO VOICE: "I have come that they may have life, and have it to the full" (John 10:10).

GROUP 1: He died and rose to set us free. *(Wrists crossed then jerked apart as though breaking chains.)*

GROUP 2: He offers a whole new start. *(Arms up and wide.)*

GROUP 3: So when we celebrate Thanksgiving Day,

ALL: Let's celebrate with a thankful heart. *(Hands over heart.)*

SONG: "For the Beauty of the Earth" *(Verse 1: Group 3; Verse 3: Groups 3 & 1; Verse Five: All)*

ALL *(slowly):* "Let the peace of Christ rule in your hearts,

GROUPS 1 & 2: "Since as members of one body

GROUPS 1 & 3: "You were called to peace.

SOLO: "And be thankful" (Colossians 3:15*).*